"THE BITTERSWEET TASTE OF THE AMERICAN DREAM"

(Emma Frances Calvin and Charles Augustus Sells)

Written by

E. Darlene Sells Treadwell

Dedicated To

My Uncle Merton Delano Sells and his wife, Grace, who cared for Grandma Em until her death.

In Memoriam (Their children)

Kenneth Leroy Sells (my dad)

Lawanda Arnell Sells Sills

Tillman Clifford Sells

Aubrey Llewellyn Sells

Martin Leonard Sells

Merton Delano Sells

To My children, Lisa, Allison and Kyle

A very special Thanks to my mom, Edith Mildred Selkridge Sells who related much of her direct experiences and these stories to her very inquisitive daughter.

ACKNOWLEDGEMENTS

Many Thanks to

Kyle Treadwell

Patrick Simmons

For their Computer Skills

And

Cinnamon O'Hara,

Document Scanning

Encouragement and Guidance

Gwinnett County Writers Guild

And

Nina Carl

Cover Design by

KECIA Y. STOVALL

FORWORD

If you are lucky enough to have great, warm, inspirational memories, and a big loving family, who love to meet, eat, laugh, joke, fellowship, and love unconditionally, then you have found Heaven and the Sells family.

Hero is a word we often hear in sports, but heroism is not always about achievements on the playing field, my heroine was located in her kitchen in Setauket, Long Island, New York..

Grandma Emma was a petite, soft-spoken woman. She was small in stature and a giant in the kitchen

This story is not a tale of woe but an inspirational expression of dreams, hopes and courage.

Hanging around Grandma Em's, house, I'd watch her stirring simmering bowls, while smells filled the air and made me eager to devour her tasty samples. When I was growing up, I thought she could have been the Black/American Indian, Julia Childs. No doubt, she was ahead of her time.

I wondered why she didn't do this for money. Through sad eyes, Grandma Em shared that her dreams almost came true in between the years of 1937 – 1949. It was a 12-year emotional merry-go-round.

Fast-forward… to the year, 2015. In today's food obsessed society, full of TV food shows; and culinary competitions, she could have launched her ideas and had a very successful career in the food industry.

Wow! I wish I had been there with her during the height of her struggles. I would have walked by her side, shoulder to shoulder, encouraging her. I'd have helped her through the corporate maze of slick talking executives and patent attorneys.

With her aspiring, inventive ideas, and food formula for "ready-to-use" corn bread mixture that were created in her Setauket kitchen, we would have pound the pavement and ridden the railroad to New York City together. If only I could have been around from 1937 – 1949! Could I have made a difference?

Grandma Em has a grandson, who is currently a Civil Attorney in Manhattan. If he had been there, would the outcome have been different? My mom, Edith Sells, told me that I was there in the 1940's with my sisters, on her lap, as she accompanied Grandma Em and her sister Edith Evans, by train from her Brooklyn brownstone to Manhattan for her appointments

I always wanted to forge deeper into this family mystery that no one ever talked about.

Many times, while I was growing up, I would pick my mom's brain for the juicy, details of grandmother's entrepreneurial adventures.

Then, I never fully grasped how those events and early disappointments affected her, in a life changing way.

It would have only been natural, to want to give up pursuing her other formulas, , after the attorneys stalling and putting her on hold, but instead. I can see in 1949 paperwork and a receipt, she submitted her new formula for vegetable cookies.

After Grandma Em's death, I was older, and married with children, but still intrigued looking for more details from Mom and Dad. They would give me bits and pieces of those long forgotten stories and try to answer the many questions I had.

For example, "Did she have a patent"? **YES**, *what was the name of her formula and product*?; **Monnies Ready-To-Use Corn Bread Mixture**; *what were the ingredients; what was the name of that sneaky baking/ flour company?*

I had a burning desire to know more, I had so many questions. I always wanted to forge deeper into this family mystery. I was going to get answers... some day.

It was in early 1991, my mom and dad were planning on moving from Long Island, New York, to Orlando, Florida. I was divorced, retired and moving to Georgia.

My dad, Kenneth, came to me and gave me this old, tattered, faded light blue, hatbox. He said, "This belonged to Grandma Em, maybe now that you have retired, you will do something with it". When my son, Kyle and I sat on the floor to explore the contents of Grandma Em's faded blue hatbox, I almost expected to smell the fragrance of my grandma's cookies when I opened that hatbox.

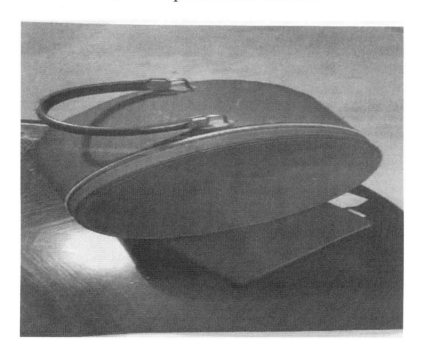

But alas, the only scent was a damp, dusty odor, emitting from the old papers, recipes, letters, documents, hidden under layers of dust, representing years of disappointments and memories.

Among grandma's carefully stored papers, I found some of the answers to my questions and burning desire to know what really happened.

There were copies of her food formulas, recipes, and letters to and from her patent attorney, corporate documents, land deeds for property out West, photos, cards, and letters. I even found her letterhead, with the name of her product, Monnies Ready-To-Use Corn Bread Mixture; her contract with the patent attorney and her patent-pending papers.

I wondered if she ever thought that some day, her children or grandchildren, would be lovingly, sorting through her treasured memories and some of the joys and challenges of her journey.

Oh, did I enjoy exploring the hatbox I had inherited!

I poured gently through the contents, with a warm, wonderful, and girlish intrigue; I scrutinized each word on the sheets of paper.

As I read each and every letter, note, contract and document, I could almost feel the hope, then the frustration, in her struggle to trust the process and the attorneys. Leaping from the pages of the letters and notes, I could feel her hurt and pain, and it touched my soul.

I desired recognition for her ingenuity, her early exploration and baking prowess. This made me more determined to get her credit and accolades. I wanted her efforts to be noted in the annals of the corporate world, the food industry, and most important, her family history and legacy.

I vacillated for years about whether to write this memoir. Would this be a discomfort for family? Would the personal family stuff upset them? Why dredge up her dusty old memories? The old days and the old dreams will never come back.

MONNIES

Ready – To – Use

Cornbread Mixture

Prepared By

Emma F. Sells　　　–　　　Setauket, N.Y

-1937-

Tel. Setauket 82

Tel. Setauket 82

MONNIES
READY-TO-USE
CORN BREAD MIXTURE
Prepared By
EMMA F. SELLS - SETAUKET, N.Y.

11/22/37

87 87
26 30
    5
6 1
   4
65

Corn Meal Mixture

g
360 — 2½ cups ^Jello corn meal fine ground
27 — 1 cup flour (unsifted) Sunfield
135 — ⅔ " fine gran ^sugar
10 — 1½ level teaspoons salt ordinary spoon
30 — 3 heaping " Baking powder (Ann
     ⎧ 8 level tablespoons dry skim ^milk
145 ⎨
     ⎩ 2 heaping " vegetable shortening Jello

2# = 3 (20g log) roughly
Emma yield figures roughly   order of mix ^ same as above
850

Yield 805 HMS mix

I let those thoughts delay me. Then I read somewhere that the word memory is from the root, "mourn".... I realized that I was mourning my grandmother's dream. So I forge on with this task of love.

I thrived on my old memories of Grandma and this adventure of hers. In some way, reminding me of my own mortality, and not completing my own dreams and tasks.

I was on fire! I wanted to get my family all together, and to do a class action suit against the flour/baking company for the stolen recipe formula. Not for revenge or retribution, I just wanted to let the world know about the loathsome, fraudulent behavior that happened, to crush my grandmother's dream. I wanted them to witness the dark side of an American dream, too. I was informed that it was way past the statute of limitations, to file a class action suit. Should I just forget about it?

I started writing letters to movie producers. I wrote to Oprah; then Tyler Perry and Spike Lee…. I wanted this lost dream of Grandma Em's, in a movie on the silver screen, have her story, shared with the world. Well, that didn't happen. I never got anyone to bring it to light in a big screen movie, or TV movie of the week or a special Hallmark movie.

I could see it as the epic saga, classic period movie. There, in the opening scene, I envisioned the railroad station, with my grandma Em's old, faded blue hatbox resting there on the railroad platform as she waited for her train to Manhattan.

My imagination floats back to 1937 and in my mind's eye, seeing my grandmother toiling away in her small kitchen, her inventive genius at work, creating the food formula that she would impart to the families of this nation. Her formula would make cooking and baking, instant, easy and tasty.

In her quiet zeal, she experimented and developed her craft, her recipes for this instant cornmeal mixture (Monnies Ready-To-Use Corn Bread Mixture) and the vegetable cookies, etal.

Disappointments and set backs at every turn. Still she would not give up. It started November 22, 1937 and dragged on until 1949.

The chemists; baking company; and patent attorney had promised to get her ready-to-use cornmeal product, to the American market place.

She traveled back and forth to New York City to keep her appointments and meetings with her patent attorney, Mr. Abraham Aaron; the chemists, Henry M. Salisbury, J.B. Staaddecker of Johnson-Salisbury, Inc., on Fifth Avenue, N.Y., NY., biscuit and flour companies right up to her last recorded correspondence in 1949.

(The following pages are her actual correspondences between 1937 and 1939).

FIFTH AVENUE HOTEL
TWENTY-FOUR FIFTH AVENUE
NEW YORK CITY

11/8/37

Dear Emma:-

Please arrange to meet me at Johnson-Salisbury, 254 West 31st N.Y. City 10th Floor Rear on Wednesday noon (Nov 10th).

Bring 6 packages of your mix and suggest you bring your Sister along. We are going ahead for you if you are willing.

Phone me to Stuyvesant 9-6400 apt. 1225 Wednesday morn about 8:30 so I'll know you will be there. Will not be home tomorrow "nite" (Tuesday) so you cannot phone me in the eve.

Cordially yours,
Jerry B Staadeker

FIFTH AVENUE HOTEL
TWENTY-FOUR FIFTH AVENUE
NEW YORK CITY

11/19/37

Dear Emma:-

Please be at Johnson-Salisbury's, 254 W 31 St 10 Floor rear on Monday afternoon (Nov 22nd) at 4:00 p.m.

Be sure to bring your Sister along.

Yours truly,
J B Staadeker

Bring your formula along for the Mix.

Johnson-Salisbury, Inc.,
& Mr. J. B. Staadecker
254 West 31st Street
New York, N.Y.

November 22nd 1937

Dear Sirs:

I wish to confirm our conversation of November 10th 1937 whereby I agreed to intrust the developement and promotion of my corn muffin and bread formula in which we were to share as follows:

    25% of profits to Johnson-Salisbury, Inc.
    25% of profits to J. B. Staadecker
    50% of profits to myself.

I wish further to give you the full rights to develope and market this formula in any manner that you deem to be to our mutual interests. Any assistance you may need I will gladly give you.

I agree to leave the whole matter to you for six months at which time if no progress has been made the formula reverts back to me, but if progress is being made at that time I agree to a six months extension of your control of the formula if you should so desire.

On this date the attached formula is turned over to you.

I hereby agree in consideration of your handling this formula that I will not discuss, use, sell or convey the formula with or to anyone during the time you are handling it, nor later if you should succeed in marketing it.

This agreement shall be binding on my successors and assigns.

    Very truly yours,

    Signed *Emma F. Sells*

    Witness *Edith Evans*
    433 Jefferson Ave. Bklyn N.Y.

Accepted by
    Date *Nov. 22 1937*

Johnson-Salisbury, Inc.

Henry M. Salisbury

Witness *Lewis Maroney*

J. B. Staadecker

    Date *Nov. 22, 1937*

Witness *Lewis Maroney*

MONNIES
READY-TO-USE
CORN BREAD MIXTURE
Prepared By
EMMA F. SELLS - SETAUKET, N. Y.

11/22/37

87
26
6
65

87
30
57
1
4

Corn Meal Mixture

2½ cups corn meal (yellow) fine ground
1 cup flour (unsifted) heaping
⅔ " sugar (fine grain)
1½ level teaspoons salt — ordinary spoon
3 heaping " Baking-powder (Ann
8 level tablespoons dry skim milk
2 heaping " vegetable shortening (Jelke)

3 (20g bg) nyly order of mix same as above
yield approx 850 roughs
yield 805 HMS mix

Virginia-Carolina Chemical Corporation

PHOSPHATE PRODUCTS DIVISION
GENERAL OFFICES RICHMOND, VA

ADDRESS REPLY DIRECT TO
NEW YORK SALES OFFICE
233 BROADWAY, NEW YORK
PHONE CORTLAND 7-3757

WORKS
CHARLESTON, S. C.

NEW YORK, N. Y.
January 4, 1938

Johnson-Salisbury Inc.,
254 West 31st Street,
New York, N.Y.

Attention: Mr. H.M. Salisbury

Gentlemen:

Referring to our conversation of yesterday, we are promptly submitting to you a 2 pound sample of our granular Lucky Leaven Monocalcium Phosphate so that you may duplicate the baking powder which you found to give you the best results, as follows -

    28% Bicarbonate of Soda
    35% Monocalcium Phosphate Granular
    37% Redried Starch.

We are also going to send you a bag of what we consider a high grade N.Y. State pancake flour.

We will probably have an exact analysis of leavening ingredients in Aunt Jamima Pancake Flour as well as a check on their gluten strength for you early next week.

As to the procedure of mixing self rising flour, we are quoting below the instructions which are commonly being followed by flour mills.

In mixing self rising flour the following points should be carefully observed:

(1) Unless flour is direct from the mill, rebolt it to remove foreign matter or lumps.

(2) Carefully weigh the flour before adding to the mixer.

(3) Do not overload the mixer - the tops of the mixing blades should show above the flour.

(4) Weigh the soda, salt, and phosphate on accurate scales. Scales should be checked.

Virginia-Carolina Chemical Corporation

PHOSPHATE PRODUCTS DIVISION
GENERAL OFFICES: RICHMOND, VA.

ADDRESS REPLY DIRECT TO
NEW YORK SALES OFFICE
233 BROADWAY, NEW YORK
PHONE CORTLAND 7-3767

WORKS
CHARLESTON, S. C.

NEW YORK, N. Y.
January 4, 1938

Johnson-Salisbury Inc.

- 2 -

    (5) Use different containers for the soda, salt, and phosphate.

    (6) Add the soda and salt to the mixer through a screened opening, and allow for thorough mixing with all of the flour. A minimum time is considered five minutes.

    (7) When the soda and salt are thoroughly mixed, add the phosphate.

    (8) Continue mixing until a thorough mix has been obtained. The efficiency of the mixer can only be determined by actual test. Each mixer has a constant time at which the best mixture is obtained. This should be determined and that time adopted as the standard for the mix. It has been found on large mixers that there is a slight tendency to unmix after the optimum mix has been obtained.

    (9) Make certain the mixer has completely discharged before adding other ingredients.

                              Very truly yours,
                       PHOSPHATE PRODUCTS DIVISION.

HMTouraine/HL

10th January 1938

Cherry,
25 Forrest Street,
Brooklyn, N.Y.

To Whom it may Concern:

Answering your advertisement in the Business Opportunity section of the New York Times dated January 9th 1938, please be advised that we have several items which we feel will meet your requirements.

If you will phone for an appointment, we will be pleased to discuss them with you.

Very truly yours,

JOHNSON-SALISBURY, INC.

1/10/39

Dear Emma:—

Just a line to advise you that Mrs Smith passed on in Hollywood and Mr Smith arrives in the morn (Tuesday) at 7:30 with the body.

She will be buried at 3:00 P.M. from Davis Undertaking Parlors in New Rochelle tomorrow (Tuesday)

Do not definitely but imagine Mr Smith will stop with me here at hotel, so if you should want to catch me, phone me here to hotel in the eve.

Cordially yours,

J B Staadeker

TELEPHONE 750

THE PAGE MILK COMPANY

SKIM MILK POWDER CHOCOLATE DRINK POWDER
WHOLE MILK POWDER CONDENSED MILK
PAGE-LAC DRY SHORTENING BUTTER
BUTTERSCOTCH POWDER SWEET CREAM

SHELBYVILLE, INDIANA

January 14, 1938

Johnson-Salisbury, Inc.
254 West 31st Street
New York, N. Y.

Gentlemen:

          We were pleased to receive your inquiry regarding our Page-Lac Shortening. We are enclosing some suggested formulae and a pamphlet describing the characteristics and uses of the product. Under separate cover, we are today mailing you a 2# sample.

          Present prices are as follows:

    1 - 4 bbl. (175# ea.) 20½¢ per lb. delivered
    5 or more barrels   19¾¢ " "   "

          We trust the sample reaches you promptly and that we may hear from you soon.

          Very truly yours,

          THE PAGE MILK COMPANY

WCH:RJMc

Enclosures: 4

FRANK R. JOHNSON
HENRY M. SALISBURY

TELEPHONE
LONGACRE 5-468

JOHNSON-SALISBURY, INC.
254 WEST 31ST STREET
NEW YORK, N. Y.

CHEMISTS
CHEMICAL ENGINEERS

January 19th 1938

Mrs. Emma F. Sells
515 Putnum Ave.,
Brooklyn, N.Y.

Dear Mrs. Sells:

I don't doubt but that you would like to know just what progress is being made with the corn bread so I am dropping you this line at this time to get you up to date.

The baking powder has been worked out so that we know the formula for compounding this on a commercial scale. We know the exact ingredients that should be put together and are not dependant on A & P.

We have run onto a very interesting product wherein the skim milk powder and the vegetable shortening are all mixed in such a manner that we can mix it easily with the other dry materials and thus do away with this most difficult part of making the mixture.

A two pound sample of this skim milk powder shortening mix should be here in the next day or so and then I will make up your entire mix and will be wanting you to come in and pass on it in a baking test here at the laboratory along with us. Everything will be then in a form suitable for submitting to a prospective purchaser of the formula.

I will drop you a line soon as this is here and let you know definately when to come in and you can let me know if the date is suitable to your convenience. We still have some of your mixture that can be baked at the same time for comparison.

Very truly yours,

JOHNSON-SALISBURY, INC.

Henry M. Salisbury

HMS/m

FRANK R. JOHNSON
HENRY M. SALISBURY

CHEMISTS
CHEMICAL ENGINEERS

TELEPHONE
LONGACRE 5-4689

JOHNSON-SALISBURY, INC.
254 WEST 31st STREET
NEW YORK, N. Y.

January 27th 1938

Mrs. Emma Sells
515 Putnum Ave.,
Brooklyn, N.Y.

Dear Mrs. Sells:

    This is to advise you that we will be ready to make a test baking of the corn bread as we have formulated it from your formula on Monday afternoon at 3:00 here at the laboratory January 31st.

    I hope that you can be here to help and pass on the product. Mr. Staadecker will be here too.

    In case you cannot make it let us know by phone and we will plan the test for some more convenient time for you.

Very truly yours,

JOHNSON-SALISBURY, INC.,

Henry M. Salisbury

HMS/m

9th February 1938

Mr. J. B. Staadecker
5th Ave., Hotel
New York, N.Y.

Dear Jerry:

The following is my price calculations on the prepared corn meal mix of Mrs. Sells.

Ingredient	Amount	Price	Cost
Fine Ground Yellow Corn Meal	360 lbs	$1.80/100#	$6.48
White Flour (Medium)	127 lbs	4½ ¢/lb	5.72
Mono Calcium Phosphate (Granular)	10.6 lbs	8¢/lb	.84
Sodium Bicarbonate	8.4 lbs	$1.75/100#	.15
Corn Starch	11.1 lbs	3.13¢/lb	.35
Salt	10 lbs	1¢/lb	.10
Fine Granulated Sugar	135 lbs	5¢/lb	6.75
PageLac	100 lbs	19 3/4 ¢/lb	19.75
Yield	762 lbs		
Cost of Materials			$40.14

Cost of Materials per lb. finished product   5¼ ¢

The Mono Calcium Phosphate, Sodium Bicarbonate and corn starch make the baking powder.

The mix is easily made by mearly mixing the weighed out products together in any mixer that will give a good agitation and which has a cover to prevent dust losses.

Trust that this finds you and Ginger much better.

As ever,

CEREALS FLOUR CORN MEAL

HOGER & CO., Inc.
PRODUCE EXCHANGE BUILDING
PHONES: WHITEHALL 4-5665-5666
NEW YORK

NO. 15264

APR 8 - 1938

SOLD TO Johnson-Salsburg, Inc.
254 West 31st Street
New York City

Terms: Net CASH

April 6, 1928

QUAN.	SIZE		BRAND AND DESCRIPTION	PRICE	AMOUNT
1	100's	Jute	Fine Yelo Bolted Meal	$2.50 Del'd	$2.50

Ex. 59 Laight Street, N.Y.C.
Delivery Order to D. L. Trucking Service
for Delivery to: Johnson-Salsburg, Inc.
254 West 31st St., N.Y.C.
10th Floor.

1991

△ Shelby Salesbook Co., Shelby, Ohio

FRANK R. JOHNSON
HENRY M. SALISBURY

TELEPHONE
LONGACRE 5-468

JOHNSON-SALISBURY, INC.
254 WEST 31st STREET
NEW YORK, N. Y.

CHEMISTS
CHEMICAL ENGINEERS

April 11th 1938

Mrs. Emma Sells
515 Putnum Ave.,
Brooklyn, N.Y.

Dear Mrs. Sells:

    I want to advise you that we have made some further tests on the corn bread and are trying to negotiate a sale with two conserns. Cannot guess as yet how they will come out.

    Mr. Staadecker is sick a-bed at this time so we cannot push as fast as we would like but we wanted you to know that things are not at a standstill.

    Trust that this finds you well and busy.

Very truly yours,

JOHNSON-SALISBURY, INC.

HMS/m

Henry M. Salisbury

June 8th 1938

Mr. B. H. Staplin
Grange League Farmers
Ithica, N.Y.

Dear Sir:

We have heard about you and your achievements and policies in the G.L.F. through a young man, H. Muller Touraine of the Virginia Carolina Chemical Co.

We are not makers of any products but do all kinds of service work on food products and at times run upon new developements which show more or less merit. Our problem generally is to find some one who is interested in them to the extent of going into production and at the same time give us a moderate return for the information which they receive from us.

At this time we are confronted with the above situation in a newly developed ceral product which we believe has an outstanding merit. I was talking this over with Mr. Touraine and he suggested that I write you to see if it would be of any interest to the G.L.F.

It is a prepared corn meal mix (Yellow Corn) that has all ingredients in it and only needs to be mixed with water in different proportions to give corn bread, corn muffins, corn pancakes and corn waffles upon baking. We have developed a mix of exceptionally fine flavor and texture in the baked product and have reason to be proud of it.

If you are interested in taking this over for your own making and marketing in package form we would be pleased to hear from you and a sample with directions for using will be sent upon your request.

In case you yourself are not interested we would appreciate any suggested outlets that you would care to suggest.

Very truly yours,
JOHNSON-SALISBURY, INC.

HMS/m

COOPERATIVE G. L. F. PRODUCTS, INC.
CHAMBER OF COMMERCE BUILDING
BUFFALO, N. Y.

June 14, 1938.

Mr. Henry M. Salisbury
Johnson-Salisbury, Inc.
254 W. 31st Street
New York, N.Y.

Dear Mr. Salisbury:

Your letter regarding your new prepared corn meal mix is acknowledged. Mr. Touraine, whom you referred to, is a splendid chap, and I miss having him drop in at the office since he has been transferred from this territory.

It seems to me that the product you have in mind should be very popular. As we have our own Experimental Kitchen in charge of Miss Lucile Brewer, who was formerly Food Specialist of the Department of Home Economics at Cornell, we are developing all of our own formulas. For this reason you can see that it would not be practical for us to consider the distribution of your product.

I would imagine that you would have a good opportunity to develop this through regular distribution channels.

Sincerely yours,

BH Staplin
Vice President
In Charge of
Purchasing & Processing

BHStaplin-d

November 30th 1939

Mr. Morris Wish
795 Crown Street
Brooklyn, N.Y.

Dear Mr. Wish:

Under separate cover I am mailing you three 20 ounce packages of the corn meal mix we have discussed.

This will give you a chance to try it out at your leisure.

I have purposely put these up in 20 ounce packages as that would be the store size of package for goods of this type.

This same mix can be used in making corn bread, corn muffins, corn pancakes and corn waffles by just varying the amount of water that they are mixed with. No other ingredient needs to be added than water.

Baking pans should be lightly greased. Baking should be done at 450°F. The bread will take about 30 to 35 minutes at this temperature. The muffins if not made too large will bake in about 25 minutes to a golden brown top. You will find the texture quite open and light. The 20 ounce package will make from 1 doz. large muffins to 18 small ones.

The dough or batter only needs enough mixing to wet it good and this should be done just before using.

The pancakes and waffles do not need any greasing of the pancake griddle or waffle iron.

The amounts of water for this size package is as follows for each item. There can be some variation form these figures of course and the following are given as a guide.

    x Corn Bread   2 Cups water
   xx Corn Muffins   1½ " "
   ½x Corn Pancakes   2½ " "
   x x Corn Waffles   2 and 3/4ths to 3 cups of water.

Will be glad to have your comments after you have tried this out.

Very truly yours,
JOHNSON-SALISBURY, INC.

(The following pages are her actual correspondences between 1940 and 1949).

FRANK R. JOHNSON
HENRY M. SALISBURY

TELEPHONE
LONGACRE 5-4689

JOHNSON-SALISBURY, INC.
254 WEST 31st STREET
NEW YORK, N. Y.

CHEMISTS
CHEMICAL ENGINEERS

January 5th 1940

Miss Emma F. Sells
Box 104
Setauket, L. I.
New York

Dear Miss Sells:

It was nice to hear from you at this time of the year, and we wish to extent to you our best wishes for this 1940.

That corn bread formula is good and for the life of me I cannot see why we have so much trouble trying to put it across. A while back I thought sure that one party was going to go ahead with it but nothing doing from him as yet.

We sure would let you know if we get anywhere with the mixture, but so far no go. Maybe this year. At least we will keep on trying. It certainly is a better formula than any on the market.

We see Mr. Staadecker now and then and are keeping him posted on anything that comes up. He said that he heard from you too at this time of the year. It is nice to be remembered.

Very truly yours,

JOHNSON-SALISBURY, INC.

Henry M. Salisbury

HMS/m

Questions to ask Lawyer

Please give me receipt where I returned the papers given me to take home.

All I want a protection for my formula. Why shouldn't I when it is not on the market yet?

If the National Biscuit has returned the formula and if not why not if they are not interested in it.

Wed. Oct. 16, 1946.

Mon. Oct. 14th 1946 I called Mr. Johnson and asked for an appointment for Wed Oct. 16 at 9 o'clock.

Kenneth and I went to his office and I asked if he would return my formula back to me. He asked the young lady who works there to look through the files and get him the paper concerning the formula. She brought him a folder containing the papers. He looked through them and gave me the formula and a few other papers but there was still quite a few left in the folder that he didn't take out. There was a circular that I gave them when I presented them the formula and he asked if he could keep it. He told me if there was anything that he could do to help me in case I should need some of the ingrediance that was needed in the mix and was unable to get it, then he would be only too glad to help me get it

ADDRESS ONLY
THE COMMISSIONER OF PATENTS

KC/lf

603-A

DEPARTMENT OF COMMERCE
UNITED STATES PATENT OFFICE
RICHMOND 20, VA.

LETTER No. 92519

August 12, 1946

Miss Emma F. Sells
267 Holsey Street
Brooklyn 16, New York

My dear Miss Sells:

    Your letter of July 6, 1946, addressed to the Superintendent of Documents has been referred to this Office for reply.

    There are no provisions under the patent laws for registering receipts or formulas and the Office cannot furnish the information requested in your letter.

                    Yours very truly

                    J. A. Brearley
                    Chief Clerk

October 25, 1946

Munn, Liddy, Glaccum & Kane, Esqs.
24 West 40th Street
New York, New York

Gentlemen:

Would you be kind enough to run a search for us whether it be copyright or patent on the following corn meal mixture:

Corn Meal Mixture

2½ cups of yellow corn meal----fine ground

1 cup of flour (unsifted) Sunnyfield A&P

2/3 cup of fine grain sugar

1½ level teaspoons of salt----ordinary spoon

3 heaping teaspoons of Baking Powder (Ann Page----A&P)

8 level tablespoons of dry skim milk

2 heaping tablespoons of vegetable shortening

order of mixing same as above

Our client has developed this corn mixture, and before attempting to place it on the market, we are desirous of knowing whether it is already being used.

Yours very truly,

SAR:RB   FISHER & RAMER

LAW OFFICES

MUNN, LIDDY & GLACCUM

24 WEST 40TH STREET

NEW YORK 18, N.Y.

October 30, 1946

ORSON DESAIX MUNN
1846-1907
CHARLES ALLEN MUNN
1865-1924
T. HART ANDERSON
1911-1939

ORSON D. MUNN
SYLVESTER J. LIDDY
JOHN H. GLACCUM

SAMUEL J. STOLL
ALFRED B. BERRY

CHRIS FEINLE
D. C. BAR

PATENT, TRADEMARK
COPYRIGHT
UNFAIR COMPETITION
FEDERAL TRADE
COMMISSION
AND
COURT OF CLAIMS
CAUSES

TELEPHONE LONGACRE 5-6400

MUNN, LIDDY, GLACCUM & RICH
1319 F. STREET, N.W.
WASHINGTON 4, D.C.

Fisher & Ramer, Esqs.,
103-10 Roosevelt Avenue,
Corona, N. Y.

Attention Mr. Ramer.

Dear Sirs:

We have your letter of October 25th setting forth a corn meal mixture.

We have not proceeded with the search for the reason that the search would not develop such a recipe. Recipes as such are not subject for statutory protection and it would be impossible to secure either a patent or a copyright on it. It follows, therefore, that a search would not develop any prior use and we will not take any action until we hear from you further.

Very truly yours,

MUNN, LIDDY & GLACCUM

By *John H Glaccum*

JHG:k

October 31, 1946

Emma F. Sells
267 Halsey Street
Brooklyn, New York

Dear Mrs. Sells:

      Will you please call to see me immediately upon the receipt of this letter.

                      Very truly yours,

                      FISHER & RAMER

SAR:RB

ABRAHAM AARON
PATENT ATTORNEY
16 Court Street
BROOKLYN, N. Y.

TRiangle 5-1626

July 20th, 1948.

Mrs. Emma F. Sells,
   267 Halsey Street, Brooklyn, 16, N.Y.,

To professional services to be rendered in preparation of application for U. S. Letters Patent for invention of "Vegetable Cookies"	$100.	
Preliminary filing fee	30.	$130.00
Received on acc't		60.00
Balance to be paid on receipt of notice of filing		$ 70.00

Aug 10/48 Rec'd on a/c   35.
Paid $35.

Balance Pd #35.
Sept. 8/48
Abraham Aaron

ABRAHAM AARON
PATENT ATTORNEY
16 COURT STREET
BROOKLYN 2, N. Y.

TRIANGLE 5-1626

July 26, 1949.

Mrs. Emma F. Sells,
Bay Shore, Long Island.

Dear Mrs. Sells:-

I have had a conversation with Mr. Curtiss of the National Biscuit Company, and at his request I have this day mailed him a copy of the Patent Application, for their consideration.

Upon receipt of any word from them, I will inform you.

Yours truly,

Abraham Aaron

But first…"identify this ingredient"…"list the quantities, measurements" …"currently testing in our kitchen and will be in touch with you"… "Come to office and bring 6 bags of the mixture with you"…, etc.

On a correspondence from Patent Attorney, Abraham Aaron, Esq. "they haven't got back to me yet"… I'm looking into it"… "I am corresponding with Mr. Strauss from the National Biscuit Company and waiting for his reply."

The pages read on and on; more delays; more postponements; and more years of stalling.

My mom, Edith, hand wrote and typed some of those letters for Grandma Em. It was pretty cool to see my now deceased mother's handwriting on those old letters. I see a handwritten note where my dad, Kenneth made an appointment after years of delay tactics, and went to the office to pick up Grandma Em's papers and files in 1949, according to her documented note… they saw more papers in the office folder but they did not return ALL of the papers from her file.

ABRAHAM AARON
PATENT ATTORNEY
16 COURT STREET
BROOKLYN 2, N.Y.

TRIANGLE 5-1626

July 26, 1949.

Mrs. Emma F. Sells,
Bay Shore, Long Island.

Dear Mrs. Sells:-

     I have had a conversation with Mr. Curtiss of the National Biscuit Company, and at his request I have this day mailed him a copy of the Patent Application, for their consideration.

     Upon receipt of any word from them, I will inform you.

Yours truly,

Abraham Aaron

ENCYCLOPEDIA of CHICAGO

Entries | Historical Sources | Maps | Special Features | User's Guide

ENTRIES : NATIONAL BISCUIT CO.

National Biscuit Co.

In 1890, Chicago lawyer Adolphus W. Green helped to found the American Biscuit Co., a large food company that took control of 40 bakeries around the Midwest. American Biscuit set up its headquarters in Chicago, where it owned three large bakeries on the city's West Side. In 1898, American Biscuit became part of the new National Biscuit Co., a 114-bakery cracker-making giant that also included the old operations of the New York Biscuit Co. National Biscuit dominated the American market for mass-produced cookies and crackers. During the first eight years of its existence, when annual sales were about $40 million, the company was based in Chicago; in 1906, the corporate headquarters was moved to New York. By 1910, National Biscuit employed nearly 1,300 men and women at its bakeries in Chicago, one of which was built especially to produce the company's popular "Uneeda" brand. By the late 1950s, when annual sales passed $400 million, National Biscuit (also known as Nabisco) still had over 1,000 workers in the Chicago area. In 1985, Nabisco was purchased by tobacco giant R. J. Reynolds but continued to operate out of the Chicago area. After 15 years of solid growth, Nabisco was purchased by another major American tobacco company, Phillip Morris (renamed Altria Group Inc. in 2003), for $19 billion. The Nabisco product line would soon fall under the operations of another Phillip Morris subsidiary, Kraft Foods of suburban Northfield. *See* Kraft Inc.

This entry is part of the Encyclopedia's Dictionary of Leading Chicago Businesses (1820-2000) that was prepared by Mark R. Wilson, with additional contributions from Stephen R. Porter and Janice L. Reiff.

Burrough, Bryan & John Helyar. **Barbarians at the Gate: The Fall of RJR Nabisco.** Harper. Jan. 1990. c.544p. illus. index. LC 89-45635. ISBN 0-06-016173-8. $22.50.

Lampert, Hope. **True Greed: What Really Happened in the Battle for RJR Nabisco.** NAL Bks. Jan. 1990. c.259p. ISBN 0-453-00719-8. $18.95.   BUS

The leveraged buyout of the RJR Nabisco Corporation for $25 billion is a landmark in American business history, a story of avarice on an epic scale. Two versions of the fierce competition for the largest buyout ever consummated are presented by skilled journalists with contrasting styles. Burrough and Helyar are clearly fascinated with the personalities of the players in the deal and with the trappings of corporate wealth. The restless, flamboyant personality of Ross Johnson, CEO of RJR Nabisco, is portrayed as the key to the events that were to unfold. The colorful description of all of the players and the events will likely have broad appeal.

Lampert signals the complexity of her story by introducing her narrative with a three-page cast of characters. Her focus on the strategy of the players and on the fast-paced action provides a more concise description of a deal big enough to augment the wealth of many rich people. Business libraries will want both versions of this story of capitalism drawn to the extreme, but students, looking for a more comprehensive treatment, will favor Lampert's version.—*Joseph Barth, U.S. Military Acad. Lib., West Point, N.Y.*

There <u>was</u> a hand-written letter to Jackie Robinson, the famous black baseball hero of her day, asking him to intercede for her. I could sense her desperation and anguish, as she realized her formula (recipe) was absconded. There was no reply from him in the hatbox.

Even with her patent pending and working directly with a patent attorney, just a simple, minute "tweak" of an ingredient, and they can say it is a new product.

Do the words trickery; thievery and fraud come to mind?

11 KEYS OF SUCCESS
Dancer Bill Robinson presents Rachel and Jackie Robinson with the 1947 Rookie of the Year prize: a new car.

*It is sometime later in 1949, (I am 7 years old) and the horrific surprise my grandmother experienced when she walked down the aisle of the local store and looked up and saw a package advertising "**instant, ready to use corn bread mixture**" on the shelf.*

My grandmother fell to her knees, in the middle of the aisle. With teary eyes, she finally saw the proof, of what she was afraid of. They had stolen her idea, her product, and her DREAM!

It is rumored in the family that the packaging of that product had the image of a black woman's face. (Was this homage to the real inventor, my grandmother Emma Frances Calvin Sells?)
We'll never know for sure. We grew up and all kids wondering if the symbol was based on our grandmother.

How do you cope with the loss? What do you do when you have lost your creation?

Grandma went back to the drawing board and back to her kitchen. Though deflated and disillusioned, she continued experimenting with her recipes and pursuing her other formulas. And I know that for sure, because you could always find my siblings and I sneaking in her Bay Shore kitchen to be her taste-testers. We would hang around the kitchen, with flour and sugar, all around us. I was often found munching the new vegetable cookies, or the baked instant corn bread mixture creations, with butter running down my sticky lips.

As I watched Grandma Em make her magical, sweet surprises, I thought of her as a scientist, a magician, and food inventor. In my mind, she was doing something really, really, special!

Even today, I can taste those beet, carrot, peas, and vegetable cookies. To date, I have not found anything like them out there in the marketplace. I savor every delicious memory of my Grandma Em and her amazing recipes.

She was so creative; to this day, I enjoy preparing her pretty green pea salad. Cold, tiny, green peas, small, pearl white onion, tossed with mayo, and served on a bed of Boston lettuce for luncheons and at all of my dinner parties. It is always great hit!

```
                    ABRAHAM AARON
                    PATENT ATTORNEY
                 16 Court Street
                    BROOKLYN, N. Y.
                    TRIANGLE 5-1626

                                    July 20th, 1948.

    Mrs. Emma F. Sells,
        267 Halsey Street, Brooklyn, 16, N.Y.,

    To professional services to be rendered in
        preparation of application for U. S. Letters
        Patent   for invention of "Vegetable Cookies"  $100.
        Preliminary filing fee                           30.   $130.00
                Received on acc't                               60.00
        Balance to be paid on receipt of notice of filing  $ 70.00
```

Vegetable Cookie Patent applied
Balance pd $35.
Sept. 8/48
Abraham Aaron

At one of our Sells Family Reunion, I did a tribute to grandma, in the form of a Recipe Cookbook with her photo on the cover and I inserted her patented recipe, formulas, inside. I then added new family recipes (from our Aunts, siblings, children and grandchildren) in the back of it, and distributed copies out to all family members in attendance. Most of the family had never seen her recipe or heard "the story".

Sometime when I was in her kitchen, waiting and watching the oven, Grandma Em would have her red journal out pasting items in it. I could see greeting cards, postcards, letters, photos and newspaper clippings and lots of interesting things I wasn't allowed to touch.

Well... I guess my interest and pride in my grandma Em showed and my Uncle Merton and his wife, Grace, presented me with Grandma Em's red journal! That same red journal I remember from way back then, many, many years ago with all those pretty postcards, letters and family photos. I couldn't wait to get home to devour the contents! I still have that red journal, and treasure that gift.

Reading every line, word, I saw first-hand, the love and admiration she had for my grandfather Charles. It just radiated from the old, browning pages. He was her pride and joy. She journaled his various trips, travel and jobs and entrepreneurial ventures. I wanted to incorporate that love in her memoir.

She had written loving things about her husband, Charles Augustus Sells.

"The best husband and father in the World", she had written.

He was one of the few if any, black business owners in the Town of Brookhaven. He was the owner of a gas station, and auto shop in East Setauket. She said he graduated from a New York Automobile School as a 1st Class Mechanic.

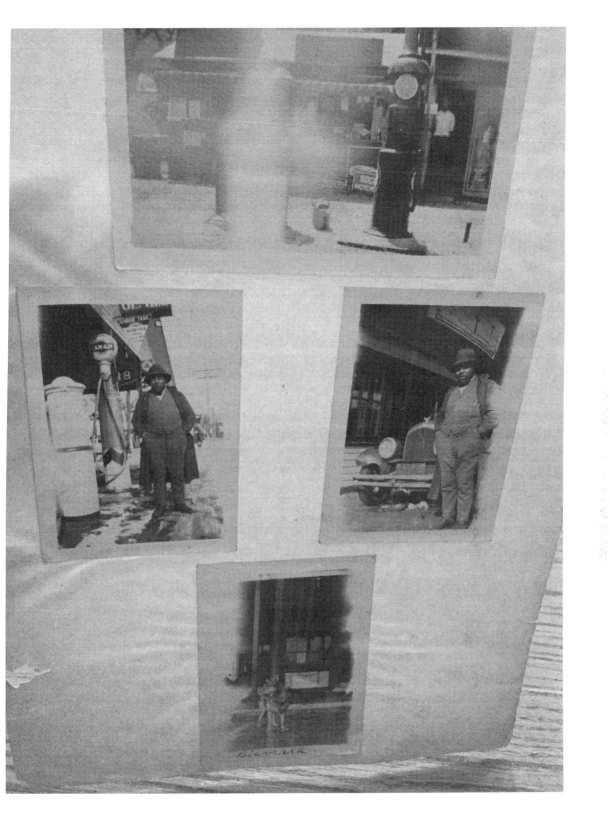

Mr. J. H. Barr Estate. Old Field

Charles Sells has accepted a position with Mr. and Mrs. James Barr, summer residents at Old Field.

When Charlie chauffeured at No

He also worked in a shipyard in Port Jefferson and owned a boat sales yard at the marina called Charlie's Boat and Tackle Station, in Setauket.

Every trip and adventure he took, she recorded and kept souvenirs, postcards, tickets, letters, and greeting cards from him. There are some tender letters written, from two sons and a daughter written especially for their Dad and she preserved them in her journal.

They are expressing their love and loyalty. It was fun to see my own Dad's childish penmanship and his personality, and his thoughts to his father.

Verified Transcript of Marriage 689 Williamson Law Book Co., Rochester 9, N.Y.

A Verified Transcript from the Register of Marriages, in the

Town of Brookhaven

COUNTY OF Suffolk, STATE OF NEW YORK

Date of Marriage January 11, 1917

Full Name of Husband Charles A Sells

His Residence Setauket, NY Age 21

Race or Color if other than White colored

Husband's Birthplace Setauket, New York

His Father's Name Grant Sells

His Mother's Maiden Name Mary A. Mills

Number of Husband's Marriages 1st

Full Name of Wife — Maiden Emma F. Calvin

Married Emma F. Calvin Sells

Her Residence at Marriage Old Field NY Age 18

Race or Color if other than White colored

Wife's Birthplace Stony Brook, NY

Her Father's Name Clifford Calvin

Her Mother's Name Abbey Phillips

Number of Bride's Marriages 1st

Name and Official Position of Person Solemnizing the Marriage
Rev. David Eato, Clergyman

Place of Marriage Setauket, New York

When Registered January 11, 1917 Register No. 1078

I hereby solemnly attest that this is a true transcript from the Public Register of Marriages as kept in Town Clerks Office

County of Suffolk and in the State Bureau of Vital Statistics of

Later Charlie went to New York to an automobile school from which he graduated a first class mechanic.

He then chauffeured for about five years, traveling all parts of the United States and was getting ready to go to Europe just when the war broke out over there and his Boss decided not to go.

Charlie then came back to Setauket, and then married Emma Calvin of Old Field, daughter of Mr and Mrs. Clifford Calvin.

rles A. Sells and Miss Emma lvin were married by the Rev. Eato, at the Bethel A. M. E. age on Thursday, Jan. 11.

Charles A. Sells and Miss Emma V. Calv were recently married by the Rev. David Eat Mr. and Mrs. Sells were tendered a recepti at the home of the groom's mother, Mrs. M. Sells, on Wednesday evening.

To My Father:

Dear Daddy:

You have always been a good father and we have never wanted for anything.

I love You Dearly

Your loving Daughter

Lavanda A. Sells

Dear Daddy —

You dont know how much I really love you. I sure do regret the times I've been bad. I know you will forgive me for such little things because you are such a good sport. I wish you would start all over in your business career again as I know there is no law agin it. I would be your right hand man because I am awful smart.

FROM — YOUR — LOVING SON

KENNETH SELLS.

Clifford's first letter to his Daddy.

from

Tillman Sells

Dear daddy
I hope you are
well and how
is Aunt annie
I wrote you
to find out
wen you are
comeing home
how is aunt
edith May
and how is
the little dog
gid by
Dear daddy
x x x x x x x x
x x x x x x x x x

When Grandma and Grandpa retired and moved to Gunther Avenue, in Bay Shore, Long Island, N.Y., my family lived very near on their property. I loved to go down the dirt path, passing the gold fishponds, and my Uncle Cliff and Aunt Dot's house, on my way to their house and the magical kitchen.

Grandpa was getting older and was a retired landscaper, who specialized in lily ponds and gold fishponds and had them around on his property. I would frequently go over to their house and check on my grandparents, especially grandfather, who was so funny and eccentric in his old age.

He had great stories and would tease us kids, unmercifully. We loved every minute of it. We loved hearing his adventures and stories, while feasting on my grandma's treats.

One of his stories, which is also documented in Grandma's journal was he was a partner with Mr. E. Cooper and Mrs. Mary Daugherty, a daredevil, female parachute jumper. He had to chauffeur Mrs. Daugherty to an Elks Convention in Detroit, Michigan

While Mrs. Daugherty was jumping from planes, my grandfather was gambling and got "beat" out of his money (hundreds of dollars in a card game).

He had only enough money to get from Detroit to Buffalo, in upstate, New York. He called home with his dilemma, and had Grandmother get money, and take a train to Buffalo, to come fetch him. They used that time as an adventure and they went to Canada and also visited Niagara Falls and other tourist attractions in Buffalo. He returned home until his next adventure.

I think that they were adventurous and had entrepreneurial spirits and were the early black history makers, and inventors, with stories that went untold, until now.

Grandpa Charles was active in civics and politics in the Town of Brookhaven. He was the Brookhaven Town Democratic Leader; he was also a Suffolk County Deputy Sheriff, and Brookhaven Town Highway Forman/Supervisor.

He was a property/land owner in both the Town of Brookhaven and the Town of Islip. In his later days, he did an interview in a Long Island Newsday newspaper. The article depicted his infamous liaison with Islip Town leader, Mr. McGowan and controversial "land deals".

As a teen, right out of school, I got my very first job and worked for Rose Jewelers in Patchogue and Grandma Em was so proud of me and assumed I was a jeweler. One day while I was visiting, she brought out her jewelry box and she thought I could tell her which was real and which was fake. I told her I would take them to my job at Rose Jewelers, and they would appraise them.

She would only give me a few at a time and I would take them back to the store and Robert or Murray would check them out and I would bring them back to her with the results. Not too good a result, most were not real, only a couple of nice opal birthstone rings.

My immediate family had 7 girls and 4 boys. My dad was Kenneth, grandma Em's first-born son.

In our teen dating years, the older girls would love go on Sunday to visit Grandma and Grandpa Sells. The boyfriends would get a "kick" out of my Grandpa Charles. He called them all "Joe", no matter what their name was, and Grandma Em would say "Charles!" and serve them a piece of her dessert of the day, as we listened to his stories.

Most of the latter years of their life, Grandpa Charles and Grandma Em, both had diabetes; and Grandpa Charles, was blind.

I remember when his sons were there trying to tell Grandpa that he could no longer drive to his favorite place, the Bay Shore Farmers Market. He was seeing double. He said, "He could still drive, because even if he saw two trees, he wasn't planning to hit either of them".

He had a special device on his phone for blind callers and a code to give to the operator, where he didn't have to dial. But he would never use or remember the code, and yell at the operators if they didn't get who he wanted, and his quote was "can't you see I am blind".

Once, when I was there, and he was upset about a political situation, he was telling the operator to get the White House, he wanted to talk to the President. I can just imagine what the operators were thinking. He was quite a character. Grandma would just say "Charles! "

I know my siblings will not forget the shoe store in his basement. When we needed shoes, Mom and Dad would send us over to Grandma and Grandpa's basement, we had to go and get measured on that metal shoe slide before he would give us our shoes. We all knew our sizes and so did he. He got the shoes at the farmer's market "closeouts" and stacked them in the basement like a shoe shop.

For the day old bakery goods he brought home from the farmer's market, Grandma would heat them in the oven to soften them and call us to the kitchen. My Grandfather would tease my sister Kay because she buttered all sides on the buns. He nicknamed her and called her "top, bottom and sides" for the longest time. Grandma Em would say "Charles!" and he would stop teasing her. I loved their playful banter.

One of my baby sisters, Jacqueline, remembers that when Grandpa was gravely ill and in the hospital, she and my sister, Candice had to go and keep Grandma company. On this occasion she said, "For dinner she made us these HUGE juicy hamburgers and piled green peas on their plates." Jacqueline whispered to Candice that "I hate peas", and that she coaxed her to hide them. She listened and shoved them under her placemat. Until this day she says, "I'm sure Grandma found them when she cleared the table, but she never said a word".

Jacqueline continued to say, "Then we all slept together in grandma's bed, and I remembered feeling that I'd never felt this close to my Grandma and tonight I felt special, and that I could comfort her in my own little way."

Grandpa Charles Augustus Sells died on July 7, 1970. Grandma Emma Frances Calvin Sells died 5 years after grandpa, on July 19, 1975.

She lived her latter years with Uncle Merton, Aunt Grace and their two sons, Merton, Jr. and Derek and final days in a nearby nursing home.

They gave us lots of laughter and stories. I loved them both so much.

NEW YORK STATE DEPARTMENT OF HEALTH BUREAU OF VITAL RECORDS
CERTIFICATE OF DEATH
TYPE ALL ENTRIES OR PRINT IN PERMANENT BLACK INK

Recorded District: 5154
Register Number: 1151

1. Name: Emma F. Sells
2. Sex: Female
3A. Date of Death: 7/19/75
3B. Hour: 10 A.M.
4. Race: Negro
5. Age: 76 yrs.
6A. Veteran: No
7A. County: Suffolk
7B. Town: Islip
7C. City or Village: Bayshore
7D. Length of Stay: 2 months
7E. Hospital or other institution: Sunrise Manor Nursing Home
8. State of Birth: New York
9. Decedent Born: 10/24/98
10. Citizen of what country: U.S.A.
11. Marital Status: Widow
13A. Usual Occupation: Housewife
13B. Kind of Business: At Home
14A. State: N.Y.
14B. County: Suffolk
14C. Town: Islip
14D. City or Village: Bayshore
14F. Street and Number: 219 Gunther Avenue
15A. Father's Name: Clifford Calvin
15B. Mother's Maiden Name: Abbie J. Phillips
16A. Informant's Name: Mr. Merton Sells
16B. Mailing Address: 234 Gunther Avenue Bayshore, New York 11706

17. PART I. Death was caused by:
(A) Arteriosclerotic Heart Disease — years
(B) General Arteriosclerosis — years

PART II. Other significant conditions: Diabetes, Hypertension, Fistula, Ramp Stump

21. Name and address of certifier: William H. Tlig M.D. 112 South Bay Ave. Brightwaters, N.Y.

22A. Burial: X
Date: 7/22/75
22B. Place of Burial: Laurel Hill Cemetery
22C. Location: Setauket, New York
23A. Funeral Home: O.B. Davis Funeral Home 218 E. Main St. Port Jefferson New York
23B. Registration No.: 00596
24A. Funeral Director: Gregory J. Bruhn
24C. Registration No.: 06472

25A. Signature of Registrar: Katherine S. Peterson, Deputy
25B. Date Filed: 7/21/75
Date Issued: 7/21/75

NEW YORK STATE DEPARTMENT OF HEALTH BUREAU OF VITAL RECORDS
CERTIFICATE OF DEATH
TYPE ALL ENTRIES OR PRINT IN PERMANENT BLACK INK.

Recorded District: 5154
Register Number: 905

1. Name: Charles A. Sells
2. Sex: Male
3A. Date of Death: 7/7/70 **3B. Hour:** 8:10 P

4. Race: Negro
5. Age: 75 yrs.
6A. Veteran of U.S. Armed Forces: No

7A. County: Suffolk
7B. Town: Islip
7C. City or Village: Bay Shore
7D. Length of Stay: 20 yrs
7E. Hospital or Other Institution: 219 Gunther Ave.

8. State of Birth: N.Y.
9. Decedent Born: 3/14/95
10. Citizen of What Country: USA
11. Marital Status: Married
12. Surviving Spouse: Emma Calvin

13A. Usual Occupation: Landscaper
13B. Kind of Business or Industry: Self employed

14A. State: New York
14B. County: Suffolk
14C. Town: Islip
14D. City or Village: Bay Shore
14E. Within Corporate Limits: Yes
14F. Street and Number: 219 Gunther Av

15A. Father's Name: Grant Sells
15B. Mother's Maiden Name: Mary Mills

16A. Informant's Name: Mrs. Emma Sells
16B. Mailing Address: 219 Gunther Ave, Bay Shore, NY 11706

PART I. 17. Death was caused by:
(A) Immediate Cause: Congestive Heart Failure — Several Mo
(B) Arteriosclerotic Heart Dis. — Unknown

PART II. Other Significant Conditions: Diabetes Mellitus

18A. Autopsy: No

20. Part I — Certifying Physician:
Signed: William Hitzig
Date: 7/7/70
From: 10/28/65 **To:** 7/7/70 **Last Seen Alive:** 7/3/70

21. Name and Address of Certifier: William Hitzig, M.D. 122 South Bay Ave, Brightwaters

22A. Burial/Cremation/Removal: Burial ☒ **Date:** 7/10/70
22B. Place of Burial: Laurel Hill Cemetery
22C. Location: Setauket, N.Y.

23A. Name and Address of Funeral Home: O.B. Davis, Inc 218 E. Main St, Port Jefferson, NY
23B. Registrar: D-0553

24A. Name of Funeral Director: Herbert L. Rueck
24B. Signature: Herbert L. Rueck
24C. 00351

25A. Signature of Registrar: Katherine S. Peterson, Deputy
25B. Date: JUL 9 1970
26A. Burial or Removal: Katherine S. Peterson, Deputy

THE OBITUARY

SELLS, CHARLES A OF 219 GUNTHER AVENUE, BAYSHORE DIED ON TUESDAY, JULY 7, 1970. BELOVED HUSBAND OF EMMA, DEVOTED FATHER OF LAWANDA A. SILLS, KENNETH, CLIFFORD AND MERTON. ALSO SURVIVED BY 17 GRANDCHILDREN, 9 GREATGRANDCHILDREN.

MR. SELLS WAS BORN IN OLD FIELD AND WAS ACTIVE IN CIVIC AND POLITICAL LIFE IN HIS EARLY YEARS. HE HAD BEEN A DEPUTY SHERIFF FOR SUFFOLK COUNTY, A FOREMAN FOR BROOKHAVEN HIGHWAY DEPARTMENT, AND A DEMOCRATIC LEADER FOR THE TOWN OF BROOKHAVEN: ALSO A MEMBER OF BETHEL A.M.E. CHURCH CLASS NO 1 HIS FAVORITE HYMNS, "O HOW I LOVE JESUS" and "WILL THERE BE ANY STARS IN MY CROWN".

SLEEP ON DEAR AND TAKE YOUR REST
WE LOVE YOU BUT GOD LOVES YOU BEST.
DONE IN SORROW
THE FAMILY

I am sure all who reads this memoir will connect with the motivating, inspirational pride I feel. Historically, it must be evident, the entrepreneurial prowess of this couple, and hopefully it would transcend to other African Americans, American Indians, other relatives of our family, community, Townships, and all of American.

Two early entrepreneurial spirits, who were certainly ahead of their time and they experienced **The Bittersweet Taste of the American Dream.**

I wanted to share their love story, for historical posterity, for their grandchildren, great grandchildren, family history and future ancestors. Perhaps, even in the annals of the big corporations and companies, to depict how the little guys were treated and out-maneuvered in the 1930's and 1940's corporate world.

Perhaps historians for The Genealogical Society; American Women in Business; African American Historical Society, American Indian Historical Society, even Civil Rights Activists who will read and research.

Here it is, 2015. I turned 73 this year, and my grandma Em's, youngest child, Merton, 80yrs old has passed away.

Where has the time gone, and what was I waiting for?
I MUST tell her story. It MUST NOT be lost forever.

There is a African American History and Culture Museum opening in the Smithsonian National Museum in Washington, DC in 2015 on the National Mall, perhaps I can send them a copy of her book with her formulas, and document the Dark side of the American Dream, that my Grandma Em experienced.

Grandma Em always had my admiration and I continue to hold her dear in my heart. Now the stories, the memories and her devastating brush with the Dark side of the American Dream is told!

Her ten (10) year runaround with the heads of the powerful American Baking Company, testing kitchens, unscrupulous chemist company and Patent Attorneys, in the American business world is told!

Alas, her "American Dream" would NOT be realized! We can only tell her story.

Bibliography

Page 41 - Excerpts / printout pages from Encyclopedia of Chicago.

Page 42,43 - Excerpts and photos from "Out of the Cracker Barrel" by William Cahn, Simon and Schuster (1969) and excerpts Pages 302,303.

Page 44 - Jackie Robinson Photo from AARP Magazine.

The following are family photos from Grandma Em's Journal

There were born five children
Emma and Charlie.
One girl and four boys.
Their names are;
[Saw]anda Arnell Sells - Born Oct. 12, 1917
[Ken]neth Leroy Sells -   " Nov. 7, 1918
[Au]brey Lluwellyn Sells - " Nov. 21, 1920
[M]artin Leonard Sells - " July, 17, 1922
[Ti]llman Clifford Sells - " Oct. 2, 1923

They have three living children
at present.
  Sawanda, Kenneth and Clifford

*13 yrs. later, son Merton Delano Sells March 18, 1933

Sixth Child, Merton Delano Sells was born Mar. 18, 1933

Family Pictures

Charlie's Mother and Uncle Frank

Kenneth Martin and Will
Nitie

Charles Augustus Sells and Emma Frances Calvin Sells (circa 1957)

Made in the USA
San Bernardino, CA
20 July 2016